POETRY FROM CRESCENT MOON

Friedrich Hölderlin: *Hölderlin's Songs of Light: Selected Poems*
translated by Michael Hamburger

Rainer Maria Rilke: *Dance the Orange: Selected Poems*
translated by Michael Hamburger

German Romantic Poetry: Goethe, Novalis, Heine, Hölderlin
by Carol Appleby

Arseny Tarkovsky: *Life, Life: Selected Poems*
translated by Virginia Rounding

Emily Dickinson: *Wild Nights: Selected Poems*
selected and introduced by Miriam Chalk

Arthur Rimbaud: *Selected Poems*
edited and translated by Andrew Jary

Arthur Rimbaud: *A Season in Hell*
edited and translated by Andrew Jary

D1603665

William Shakespeare: *The Sonnets*
edited and introduced by Mark Tuley

Edmund Spenser: *Heavenly Love: Selected Poems*
selected and introduced by Teresa Page

Robert Herrick: *Delight In Disorder: Selected Poems*
edited and introduced by M.K. Pace

John Donne: *Air and Angels: Selected Poems*
selected and introduced by A.H. Ninham

D.H. Lawrence: *Being Alive: Selected Poems*
edited with an introduction by Margaret Elvy

Percy Bysshe Shelley: *Paradise of Golden Lights: Selected Poems*
selected and introduced by Charlotte Greene

Thomas Hardy: *Her Haunting Ground: Selected Poems*
edited, with an introduction by A.H. Ninham

Emily Bronte: *Darkness and Glory: Selected Poems*
selected and introduced by Miriam Chalk

Henry Vaughan: *A Great Ring of Pure and Endless Light: Selected Poems*
selected and introduced by A.H. Ninham

Sex-Magic-Poetry-Cornwall: A Flood of Poems
by Peter Redgrove, edited with an essay by Jeremy Mark Robinson

BOOKS BY URSULA LE GUIN

NOVELS

Rocannon's World
City of Illusions
Planet of Exile
A Wizard of Earthsea
The Left Hand of Darkness
The Tombs of Atuan
The Lathe of Heaven
The Farthest Shore
The Dispossessed: An Ambiguous Utopia
Very Far Away from Anywhere Else
The Word for World is Forest
The Eye of the Heron
Malafrena
The Beginning Place (a.k.a. *Threshold*)
Always Coming Home
Tehanu: The Last Book of Earthsea
The Telling
The Other Wind
Gifts
Voices
Powers
Lavinia

POETRY

Wild Angels
Walking in Cornwall: A Poem for the Solstice
Hard Words, and Other Poems
Wild Oats and Fireweed
Going Out With Peacocks and Other Poems
The Twins, the Dream / Las Gemelas, El Sueño,
    with Diana Bellessi
Sixty Odd: New Poems
Incredible Good Fortune

COLLECTED SHORT STORIES

The Wind's Twelve Quarters
Orsinian Tales
The Compass Rose
Buffalo Gals and Other Animal Presences
A Fisherman of the Inland Sea
Four Ways to Forgiveness
Searoad
Unlocking the Air and Other Stories
Tales from Earthsea
The Birthday of the World and Other Stories
Changing Planes

OTHER WRITING

From Elfland to Poughkeepsie
Dreams Must Explain Themselves
Torrey Pines Reserve
In the Red Zone, with Hank Pander
The Blind Geometer / The New Atlantis,
        with Kim Stanley Robinson
Dancing at the Edge of the World: Thoughts on Words,
        Women, Places
Fire and Stone, with Laura Marshall
Blue Moon over Thurman Street
Edges, with Virginia Kidd
The Enchanted Landscape: Photographs 1940-1975,
        with Wynn Bullock
The Language of the Night: Essays on Fantasy and Science Fiction
Myth and Archetype in Science Fiction
Talk about Writing
Findings
Tao Te Ching, by Lao Tzu
Steering The Craft
The Way of the Water's Going: Images of the Northern
        California Coastal Range
The Wave in the Mind
Cheek By Jowl

FOR CHILDREN

Leese Webster
Solomon Leviathan's 931st Trip Around the World
A Visit from Dr. Katz
Catwings
Catwings Return
Fish Soup
A Ride on the Red Mare's Back
Wonderful Alexander and the Catwings
Tom Mouse and Ms. Howe
Jane On Her Own
Cat Dreams

URSULA LE GUIN

Born in 1929 in Berkeley, California, Ursula Le Guin is the daughter of the writer Theodora Kroeber and anthropologist Alfred Kroeber. She studied at Radcliffe College and Columbia University. Since 1958, Le Guin has lived in Portland, Oregon, with her husband Charles Le Guin, whom she married in Paris in 1953. She has three children, and three grandchildren.

Ursula Le Guin has written novels, poetry, children's books, essays and translations. Le Guin's most well-known works are her *Earthsea* fantasies, and her science fiction novels, such as *The Left Hand of Darkness, The Dispossessed* and *Always Coming Home*. She also has eleven collections of short stories, six poetry books, and eleven books for children (including the *Catwings* books). Le Guin's books have received the National Book Award, five Hugo Awards, five Nebula Awards and the Kafka Award, among many others, and have been finalists for the Pulitzer Prize and American Book Award.

Walking In Cornwall

Paul Lewin, *Robin's Rocks, Cornwall*

Walking In Cornwall

Ursula Le Guin

CRESCENT MOON

First published 1976. Third edition 2012.
© Ursula Le Guin 1976, 2012.

Printed and bound in the United States.
Set in Palatino 11 on 14pt.
Designed by Radiance Graphics.

British Library Cataloguing in Publication data

Le Guin, Ursula K., 1929-
Walking In Cornwall
I. Title
811.5'4.

ISBN-13 9781861713919 (Hbk)
ISBN-13 9781861713681 (Pbk)

Crescent Moon Publishing
P.O. Box 1312
Maidstone, Kent
ME14 5XU, Great Britain
www.crmoon.com

CONTENTS

Paul Evans, *The Brisons*

ACKNOWLEDGEMENTS

Thanks to Vaughne Hansen.

For the illustrations thanks to Paul Evans, Paul Lewin, Great Atlantic Map Works Gallery, St Just, Cornwall, and Michael Jay.

Illustrations © Paul Evans. Paul Lewin.

www.ursulakleguin.com
www.paullewin.co.uk
www.paulevans-artist.com

Paul Evans, *Priest Cove*, 2006

Walking In Cornwall

CHÛN

———

The first day to the high place of Chûn.
The road goes low between walls
of spark-strown granite, dry-laid
by those who cleared the little fields,
and kept up since, for maybe eighty generations:
heavy boulders earthset as the base,
smaller rocks set close and vertical.
Gorse breaks gold from roots among the rocks.
The road stinks, till we get past
a farmer turning muck on his high field.
The farmyard drive's all liquid mud. Then no road,
only a grass track up the hill
and up, and wind a bit, and all the while the land
rising in long green swells wave-netted by the walls
that mark the oldest fields in England,
and up, onto the land into the wind,
until we realise that this shallow ditch
between rockheaps and gorse and heather clumps
is the outer ring, and we have come to Chûn.
  The inner ring still stands. Dry stones.
There are some roofless rooms. The heather bells
are last year's, dry and snakeskin-frail.
A lark goes up and up and sings and sings
over the fortress of the sea-wind.
Two big stones mark the gateway,
and the wind drives bright between them,
king of the castle, coming home.
        The well

waits. Clear water under rocks,
slipped coping-boulders, knots of weeds.
A hilltop spring, that made the place
defensible, a living-place: the life of Chûn,
secret and perfectly clear. As clear as breath.
    We made a little offering to the spring,
eating our picnic: a bit of pastry and an apple core:
you offer to such places. Then you hope
they know it wasn't meant as litter.
    Straight on from the standing stones
of the northwest gateway, past the view
to Morvah and the dull gleam of the sea,
over the granite backbone of the land
to Chûn Quoit. Here's a grave turned inside out.
They set the stone slabs up, set the great roofstone on,
laid the bodies in the room of rock,
piled the earth all over in a mound,
a rounded barrow. And grass and gorse and heather
grew over all, no doubt. But roots
have trouble holding, in a wind
that blows across five thousand miles of sea
for twenty centuries. The covering earth's
all gone, the bones are gone; the grave
itself stands up, grey granite in the wind.
There's not a soul, there's not a sound.
Sun's gold on the old stones.
Lichen is lovely, grey-green, violet, gold.
Clouds drift and pile up, grey, grey-blue, and white.
They pass on southward on the wind
over the high place, over the old place,
the rock-wall rings, the grave, the shallow well.

Chûn is a name
in a tongue that no one speaks now
but rocks and larks.

Paul Evans, *Cornish Field Flowers, Near Sennen*, 2006

MÊN-AN-TOL, THE NINE MAIDENS, DINGDONG MINE, AND LANYON QUOIT

———

We passed Woon Gumpus Common on the left.
You can't go everywhere,
even when it's called Woon Gumpus.

Four Americans straggling on a heath.

The track's a dry streambed. Little signs
point softly, rain and weather-faded,
whisper: Mên-an-Tol.

> The ring is in the valley
> the door is in the valley
> the valley is the mother
>
> Round door
> open mouth
> hollow thing
>
> Time passes through time's circle
>
> The mother wears this ring
>
> What is the marrow of this bone?
>
> Down in the hollow valley

come be born
of stone

O it is the quietest place,
the shallow valley, Mên-an-Tol.

Then up again and through the buckskin bracken
and March blows blithely off the prancing ocean
and makes all noses run, and up we go
and find nine maidens where the map says none:
old maidens, low and lumpy; some have fallen,
some got staggering drunk in 99 B.C.
Small maidens, very old, not saying much.
On past them; and the topmost crest and spine
of this hard granite ridge, this skin-on-bone,
this high-and-dry place, turns to bog:
the springs rise everywhere. Boots squelch.
We hop from gorse to tussock,
and so arrive at where the map says nine,
and there they are. We count them as eleven,
or maybe twelve. Maybe you can't count them
twice the same. You can't be sure of maidens.
And when they dance in rings in early March
in lonely places, you must count the sun
among their number.

Ring around the sun O
Sun among the ring
Nine and nine are one O
So stones sing.

So on we go and up and overland
a little farther to the sober thing,
the upstart and admonitory finger,
the chimney of the tin mines on the hill.

It's made of the same stuff as Chûn,
the Maidens, Mên-an-Tol, but not in rings:
These stones are cut, cut square,
and set to stay there, grand the building, and it
                              stayed,
though all the shafts have sunk in, dimpled pits,
and you can only guess at where the wheels worked
                              once,
the noise of iron gears, the sluice's rush,
the glare of smelting, women sorting ore,
men who used to sweat here underfoot,
down in the hollow places in the dark.
All quiet now, up here; all gone to grass;
the tin mined out; the miners have gone home.

The Isles of Tin, the Misty Isles!
"It was not certain," Caesar says, "that *Britannia*
existed, till I went there."

Nothing is certain, Caesar bach.

Nine maidens sort the misty ore
at full moon in the shadow of the tower.

On down and down now, through the
                    pasturelands.
Ten young heifers (is it nine? or twelve?)
stare with the eyes of anxious goddesses
and heave warm, muddy, ruddy flanks
in sighs as we go by, excuse us please
for walking through your pasture to the Quoit.
This one is Lanyon. We have left cut stone
a thousand years ahead of us again.
Lanyon's so big you can walk under it.
The stones have soaked up sun and are as warm

as heifer's flanks. Once it was chilly here,
and dark, under the barrow; but the barrow's gone,
the wind blows through the sunlit tomb.
All's dry and clear and clean. You cannot count
the years. Counting means nothing here.
Measure a ring's length, count the sun!
Can you weigh emptiness?

The valleys are shallow
and the hills hollow
at the triple ring of Chûn
at the ring of Mên-an-Tol
at the rings of the Nine Maidens.
The empty mineshaft and the open grave
are full of sunlight
and the wind is sweet as honey in the mouth.

Paul Lewin, *Hella Point*, 2006

CASTLE AN DINAS AND CHYSAUSTER VILLAGE

———

The next day: off the humping bus
up past the quarry. Danger!
Blasting: Weekdays at Noon.
White sandhills, lunar; then a gulf, a gap.
A big blast it was made that one –
a hole so big you see the ocean through it.
Hurry on by, they might just blow us up.

There on top of things is Roger's Tower.

Who on earth was Roger? Bishop, prince?
Landgrave of Ludgvan? Emperor of St. Erth?
Why did he build his Tower? No one knows.
It looms up here for miles, a great keep,
a mighty ruin on the vaulting hill;
you get there, and it's all of twelve feet high.
Never was higher. Four fat little turrets
complete its whole ambition.
Two men might fit inside it,
if they had not been eating Cornish cream.
Around behind it, ruinous,
and breaking into yellow gorse-flame everywhere,
the rings, Chûn's sister, Castle An Dinas.
So here's the Bronze Age, and in front of it
the Middle Ages. Here's the granite walls
(boulders for base, small stones set vertical)
and here's the granite walls (cut square, set true).

And who were they? and who was Roger? who?
the wind says to the heather.
Elegant, the arch above the door.
And no one knows what Roger's Tower's for.

Place is three fourths of Time.

So we went down, and missed the muddy path
across the fields, and trudged along the road
for decades, and the back of my right knee
objected, ligament by ligament,
and Theo lagged, until the brindle cat
of Little Chysauster Farm came out and purred
and wanted to be petted till the cows came home,
which cheered us up; and we went on, and climbed
past stone-walled fields, zigzag,
hungry and hot and tired, and came home.

It was home, once, Chysauster village was.
Nine families, their cattle, their hearthfires.

O small cold hearths, so old, so old,
yet you could light a fire in them tonight.
It would be the same fire.
We don't need very much:
water and warmth and walls, the flickering ring of
                              faces.

There is a room as round as any coin
and filled brimful with sunlight.
That was a woman's room, I think.

The roofs are off, the wooden walls are gone,
the centerposts are gone, but not the hollowed stones.

There was a spring ran through the half-walled court
of one of the nine houses, in a chute of stone.
The spring went dry. No sound but wind.
Although you kneel beside the little hearths
you cannot hear the arguments,
the stories, or the snores on winter nights.
But if you sat a while in the round room
you might hear, I don't know, you might –
a woman singing to a sleepy child.

A woman singing softly. Now and then.

The laughter of my children
far off among the ways among the stones.

The laughter of her children.

And the wind as sweet as honey in the mouth.

Paul Lewin, *Zawn Kellys*, 2006

URSULA LE GUIN

BIBLIOGRAPHY OF POETRY

Wild Angels, Capra Press, Santa Barbara, CA, 1974

Walking in Cornwall, chapbook, 1976

Tillai and Tylissos, with Theodora Kroeber, Red Bull, 1979

Hard Words and Other Poems, Harper & Row, New York, NY, 1981

In the Red Zone, with Henk Pander, Lord John, 1983

Buffalo Gals and Other Animal Presences, Capra Press, Santa
    Barbara, CA, 1987

Wild Oats and Fireweed: New Poems, Harper & Row, New York,
    NY, 1988

No Boats, Ygor & Buntho Make Books Press, 1992

Blue Moon over Thurman Street, with Roger Dorband, New Sage,
    1993

Going Out With Peacocks and Other Poems, HarperCollins, New
    York, NY, 1994

*The Twins, The Dream: Two Voices / Las Gemelas, El Sueño: Dos
    Voces,* with Diana Bellessi, Arte Público Press, Houston, TX,
    1996

Sixty Odd, Shambhala, 1999

Incredible Good Fortune: New Poems, Shambhala, 2006

Paul Evans, *Cape Cornwall*

Paul Lewin, *Pendeen Old Cliff*, 2002

CRESCENT MOON PUBLISHING

web: www.crmoon.com e-mail: cresmopub@yahoo.co.uk

ARTS, PAINTING, SCULPTURE

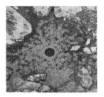

The Art of Andy Goldsworthy
Andy Goldsworthy: Touching Nature
Andy Goldsworthy in Close-Up
Andy Goldsworthy: Pocket Guide
Andy Goldsworthy In America
Land Art: A Complete Guide
The Art of Richard Long
Richard Long: Pocket Guide
Land Art In the UK
Land Art in Close-Up
Land Art In the U.S.A.
Land Art: Pocket Guide
Installation Art in Close-Up
Minimal Art and Artists In the 1960s and After
Colourfield Painting
Land Art DVD, TV documentary
Andy Goldsworthy DVD, TV documentary
The Erotic Object: Sexuality in Sculpture From Prehistory to the Present Day
Sex in Art: Pornography and Pleasure in Painting and Sculpture
Postwar Art
Sacred Gardens: The Garden in Myth, Religion and Art
Glorification: Religious Abstraction in Renaissance and 20th Century Art
Early Netherlandish Painting
Leonardo da Vinci
Piero della Francesca
Giovanni Bellini
Fra Angelico: Art and Religion in the Renaissance
Mark Rothko: The Art of Transcendence
Frank Stella: American Abstract Artist
Jasper Johns
Brice Marden
Alison Wilding: The Embrace of Sculpture
Vincent van Gogh: Visionary Landscapes
Eric Gill: Nuptials of God
Constantin Brancusi: Sculpting the Essence of Things
Max Beckmann
Caravaggio
Gustave Moreau
Egon Schiele: Sex and Death In Purple Stockings
Delizioso Fotografico Fervore: Works In Process 1
Sacro Cuore: Works In Process 2
The Light Eternal: J.M.W. Turner
The Madonna Glorified: Karen Arthurs

LITERATURE

J.R.R. Tolkien: The Books, The Films, The Whole Cultural Phenomenon
J.R.R. Tolkien: Pocket Guide
Tolkien's Heroic Quest
The *Earthsea* Books of Ursula Le Guin
Beauties, Beasts and Enchantment: Classic French Fairy Tales
German Popular Stories by the Brothers Grimm
Philip Pullman and *His Dark Materials*
Sexing Hardy: Thomas Hardy and Feminism
Thomas Hardy's *Tess of the d'Urbervilles*
Thomas Hardy's *Jude the Obscure*
Thomas Hardy: The Tragic Novels
Love and Tragedy: Thomas Hardy
The Poetry of Landscape in Hardy
Wessex Revisited: Thomas Hardy and John Cowper Powys
Wolfgang Iser: Essays and Interviews
Petrarch, Dante and the Troubadours
Maurice Sendak and the Art of Children's Book Illustration
Andrea Dworkin
Cixous, Irigaray, Kristeva: The *Jouissance* of French Feminism
Julia Kristeva: Art, Love, Melancholy, Philosophy, Semiotics and Psychoanalysis
Hélene Cixous I Love You: The *Jouissance* of Writing
Luce Irigaray: Lips, Kissing, and the Politics of Sexual Difference
Peter Redgrove: Here Comes the Flood
Peter Redgrove: Sex-Magic-Poetry-Cornwall
Lawrence Durrell: Between Love and Death, East and West
Love, Culture & Poetry: Lawrence Durrell
Cavafy: Anatomy of a Soul
German Romantic Poetry: Goethe, Novalis, Heine, Hölderlin
Feminism and Shakespeare
Shakespeare: Love, Poetry & Magic
The Passion of D.H. Lawrence
D.H. Lawrence: Symbolic Landscapes
D.H. Lawrence: Infinite Sensual Violence
Rimbaud: Arthur Rimbaud and the Magic of Poetry
The Ecstasies of John Cowper Powys
Sensualism and Mythology: The Wessex Novels of John Cowper Powys
Amorous Life: John Cowper Powys and the Manifestation of Affectivity (H.W. Fawkner)
Postmodern Powys: New Essays on John Cowper Powys (Joe Boulter)
Rethinking Powys: Critical Essays on John Cowper Powys
Paul Bowles & Bernardo Bertolucci
Rainer Maria Rilke
Joseph Conrad: *Heart of Darkness*
In the Dim Void: Samuel Beckett
Samuel Beckett Goes into the Silence
André Gide: Fiction and Fervour
Jackie Collins and the Blockbuster Novel
Blinded By Her Light: The Love-Poetry of Robert Graves
The Passion of Colours: Travels In Mediterranean Lands
Poetic Forms

POETRY

Ursula Le Guin: Walking In Cornwall
Peter Redgrove: Here Comes The Flood
Peter Redgrove: Sex-Magic-Poetry-Cornwall
Dante: Selections From the Vita Nuova
Petrarch, Dante and the Troubadours
William Shakespeare: Sonnets
William Shakespeare: Complete Poems
Blinded By Her Light: The Love-Poetry of Robert Graves
Emily Dickinson: Selected Poems
Emily Brontë: Poems
Thomas Hardy: Selected Poems
Percy Bysshe Shelley: Poems
John Keats: Selected Poems
Joh n Keats: Poems of 1820
D.H. Lawrence: Selected Poems
Edmund Spenser: Poems
Edmund Spenser: Amoretti
John Donne: Poems
Henry Vaughan: Poems
Sir Thomas Wyatt: Poems
Robert Herrick: Selected Poems
Rilke: Space, Essence and Angels in the Poetry of Rainer Maria Rilke
Rainer Maria Rilke: Selected Poems
Friedrich Hölderlin: Selected Poems
Arseny Tarkovsky: Selected Poems
Arthur Rimbaud: Selected Poems
Arthur Rimbaud: A Season in Hell
Arthur Rimbaud and the Magic of Poetry
Novalis: Hymns To the Night
German Romantic Poetry
Paul Verlaine: Selected Poems
Elizaethan Sonnet Cycles
D.J. Enright: By-Blows
Jeremy Reed: Brigitte's Blue Heart
Jeremy Reed: Claudia Schiffer's Red Shoes
Gorgeous Little Orpheus
Radiance: New Poems
Crescent Moon Book of Nature Poetry
Crescent Moon Book of Love Poetry
Crescent Moon Book of Mystical Poetry
Crescent Moon Book of Elizabethan Love Poetry
Crescent Moon Book of Metaphysical Poetry
Crescent Moon Book of Romantic Poetry
Pagan America: New American Poetry

MEDIA, CINEMA, FEMINISM and CULTURAL STUDIES

J.R.R. Tolkien: The Books, The Films, The Whole Cultural Phenomenon
J.R.R. Tolkien: Pocket Guide
The *Lord of the Rings* Movies: Pocket Guide
The Cinema of Hayao Miyazaki
Hayao Miyazaki: *Princess Mononoke*: Pocket Movie Guide
Hayao Miyazaki: *Spirited Away*: Pocket Movie Guide
Tim Burton : Hallowe'en For Hollywood
Ken Russell
Ken Russell: *Tommy*: Pocket Movie Guide
The Ghost Dance: The Origins of Religion
The Peyote Cult
Cixous, Irigaray, Kristeva: The *Jouissance* of French Feminism
Julia Kristeva: Art, Love, Melancholy, Philosophy, Semiotics and Psychoanalysis
Luce Irigaray: Lips, Kissing, and the Politics of Sexual Difference
Hélene Cixous I Love You: The *Jouissance* of Writing
Andrea Dworkin
'Cosmo Woman': The World of Women's Magazines
Women in Pop Music
HomeGround: The Kate Bush Anthology
Discovering the Goddess (Geoffrey Ashe)
The Poetry of Cinema
The Sacred Cinema of Andrei Tarkovsky
Andrei Tarkovsky: Pocket Guide
Andrei Tarkovsky: *Mirror*: Pocket Movie Guide
Andrei Tarkovsky: *The Sacrifice*: Pocket Movie Guide
Walerian Borowczyk: Cinema of Erotic Dreams
Jean-Luc Godard: The Passion of Cinema
Jean-Luc Godard: *Hail Mary*: Pocket Movie Guide
Jean-Luc Godard: *Contempt*: Pocket Movie Guide
Jean-Luc Godard: *Pierrot le Fou*: Pocket Movie Guide
John Hughes and Eighties Cinema
Ferris Bueller's Day Off: Pocket Movie Guide
Jean-Luc Godard: Pocket Guide
The Cinema of Richard Linklater
Liv Tyler: Star In Ascendance
Blade Runner and the Films of Philip K. Dick
Paul Bowles and Bernardo Bertolucci
Media Hell: Radio, TV and the Press
An Open Letter to the BBC
Detonation Britain: Nuclear War in the UK
Feminism and Shakespeare
Wild Zones: Pornography, Art and Feminism
Sex in Art: Pornography and Pleasure in Painting and Sculpture
Sexing Hardy: Thomas Hardy and Feminism

The Light Eternal is a model monograph, an exemplary job. The subject matter of the book is beautifully
organised and dead on beam. (Lawrence Durrell)
It is amazing for me to see my work treated with such passion and respect. (Andrea Dworkin)

CRESCENT MOON PUBLISHING
P.O. Box 1312, Maidstone, Kent, ME14 5XU, Great Britain. www.crmoon.com

cresmopub@yahoo.co.uk   www.crescentmoon.org.uk

Made in the USA
San Bernardino, CA
25 January 2018